Journey through

THURINGIA

Photos by
Tina and Horst Herzig

Text by
Ernst-Otto Luthardt

Stürtz

First page:
*Sausages – and dump-
lings – are the Thuringians'
favourite food. The proper*

*way to cook them is not
fried in a pan but
barbecued on a grill.*

Previous page:
*The cathedral in combina-
tion with St Severi is
Erfurt's local landmark.
The cathedral was first*

*mentioned in 1117 as the
church of St Mary's.
St Severi is one of the best
Gothic places of worship
in Germany.*

Below:
*There's nothing to compare
with this north of the Alps:
the Krämerbrücke river*

*crossing in Erfurt, lined
with splendid half-
timbered houses and
even a church.*

Page 10/11:
High up above the town of
Eisenach, spread out
along a rocky spur, is
Wartburg Castle, with
marvellous views of the
Thuringian Forest. Most
of its buildings date back
to the 19th century; here,
part of the great hall.

Contents

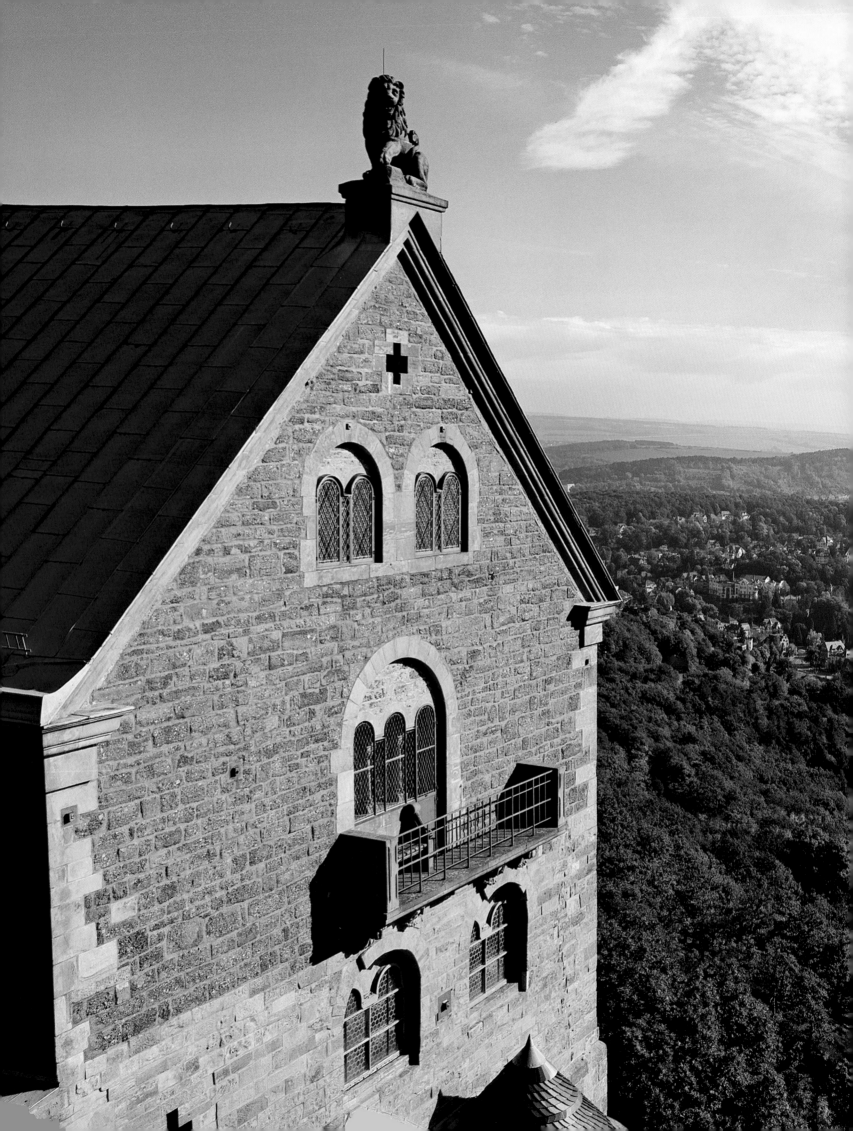

Thuringia – stories and histories

The residence of the princes of Schwarzburg-Sondershausen, surrounded by an informally landscaped garden, bears traces of the architectural fads of no less than seven centuries. This fountain tinkles outside the west wing with its baroque embellishments.

The kingdom of the Thuringii was destroyed near Burgscheidungen by the Franks and Saxons in 531. Its territories subsequently became the subject of much haggling, changing hands time and again. The potentates of the day developed a taste for the diminutive, separating and partitioning when there was actually nothing much left to divide. *"A patch of blue and brown, a little red, yellow, green, just a tiny amount of each, here a drop, there a dash, ever greater and ever smaller, so that it is a confusion of colour. One portion may be called Prussia or Hesse or Bavaria, almost a dozen little countries are called Saxony; here a Hildburghausen, a Sangerhausen, a Sondershausen, there the tiny territory of Reuß with Greiz, Schleiz, Lobenstein"* is how one 19th-century historian described the situation. The map of Germany was as bright as a parrot – but nowhere more vibrant than in the lands of the Thuringians, chiefly ruled by the Wettins of Saxony and their successors.

The land seem doomed to an eternity of war between feuding family members over matters of succession, with ever more divisions the result. Yet out of this political sump surprisingly great things emerged, particularly with regard to literature, art and music. Minute Weimar became a veritable temple of the Muses and intellectual thought. Other small towns were also much talked about, where any princeling worth his salt founded a private orchestra. One of these was at the Schwarzburgischer Hof in Sondershausen; the original military band metamorphosed into the Loh-Orchester, famous for its promotion of the New German School of music and directed by Max Bruch for a time. In Sachsen-Meiningen Duke Georg II (1826–1914) personally catapulted his theatrical company to world fame, their performances then considered exemplary and still a source of inspiration to modern theatre.

A state of Thuringia was created in 1920 but survived only for a brief period. Now that the German nation is no longer divided, the 'green heart of Germany' can again beat with renewed vigour in its rightful place.

Spring awakening

When spring comes to Thuringia, it first kisses the valley of the Saale near Jena. The tall slopes of Muschelkalk that line the river store the early warmth. This is beneficial to the many steppe plants which have survived here although they have disappeared from regions with less favourable climates. Jena thus boasts one of the most prolific natural habitats of the orchid in Germany. The arrival of the floral year is heralded by the purple pasque flower, followed by the lady's slipper and common spotted orchid, the early coralroot and Orchis purpurea, one of the prettiest of the local orchids. Experts – who out of necessity are also protectors of these delicate plants – know where to find a whole host of flowers, many of them endangered species. These include the lizard orchid, whose large lips twist like a corkscrew, and Epipactis rubiginosa that smells of chocolate. Liverwort, violets, lily of the valley, Turk's cap lily and honeysuckle carpet fields and forests, with tufts of perennial grass sprouting from the slopes. This extremely robust plant can even reroot itself, sliding down the hillside to its new position with the mud and scree.

The vegetation of the steppe heath is low-growing and more modest, its true beauty not immediately apparent. Some species rely on strength in numbers, such as the St Bernhard's lily. When clumps of *Anthericum liliago* open up their tiny star-shaped flowers, it's as if the winter has again covered the ground with snow. Many shrubs and bushes are also smothered in blossom, with the Guelder rose and sloe decked out in sparkling white, their fruits later brilliant red and a deep blue. The horticultural spectrum is further complemented by the crimson petals and hips of the wild rose.

The surrounding villages of Ziegenhain, Lobeda and Drackendorf, now part of Jena, are popular hiking terrain. None other than Johann Wolfgang von Goethe once paid them a visit, drawing inspiration from the misty riverside meadows between Jena and Kunitz to pen his poem the *Erlkönig* or erlking.

The state capital

In 742 missionary St Boniface described Erfurt in a letter to the pope. Legend has it that here he felled Donar's holy oak in order to demonstrate to the heathens the impotence of the old religion. The lofty spires of the cathedral and St Severi later arose where the tree had once stood. Erfurt is a prime example of how cities evolved in the Holy Roman Empire. The new elite were the city's craftsmen and merchants who abhorred local impoverished knights trying to seize a portion of municipal wealth

Haus zum Breiten Herd, erected at the end of the 16th century in the Renaissance style, is one of the most splendid town houses in Erfurt. The 'painted' ladies under the window depict the five senses.

through robbery, murder and manslaughter. When in 1289 King Rudolf of Habsburg proclaimed a general state of peace at the imperial diet of Erfurt, he and Erfurt's citizens went forth and slighted the strongholds of Thuringia's robber-barons.

Meister Eckhart of Hochheim, born near Gotha in c.1260 and made a Dominican Erfurt prior and provincial superior when still under 30, preferred to build rather than destroy confidence. He told his flock *"You have a part in God, you yourselves are godly … you are royally free, you own the same and more than the emperor and pope."* His words bore both economic and academic fruit; Erfurt was transformed into a centre of trade for both tangible commodities and scholarly ideas. In 1392 one of the first universities in Germany opened its doors in the city, where circles of learned Humanists led by writer Helius Eobanus Hessus and later rector Johann Crotus or Crotus Rubeanus keenly battled against the power of stupidity.

The prettiest streets in town are those that take us back in time. The Krämerbrücke across the river, lined on both sides with half-timbered houses and even a church, is second to none north of the Brenner Pass. The baroque legacy of the Electorate of Mainz is also worthy of closer attention. The absolute jewels in the crown of Old Erfurt, however, are the town houses built in the spirit of the late Gothic and early Renaissance, with names such as Zur Hohen Lilie (The High Lily), Zum Güldenen Hecht (The Golden Pike) and Zum Roten Stern (The Red Star) both evocative and slightly mysterious.

The peasants revolt

It happened just as depicted on Werner Tübke's panorama at the memorial in Bad Frankenhausen on the morning of May 15, 1525: rebellious peasants, salt workers and saltworks owners and tenants, miners, travelling journeymen and escaped monks who had dug themselves in behind a barricade of wagons were attacked by the royal army and brutally slaughtered. The White Mountain was drowned in blood and thereafter known as Schlachtberg or Battle Hill. Before battle commenced Thomas Müntzer, the leader of Thuringia's peasants, believed he had received a sign from God: *"Do you see that rainbow in the sky? It means that God wishes to help us, we who bear the rainbow on our banner, against the murderous princes and that he threatens*

EN HERD

them with judgement and punishment. *Thus be not afraid*", he encouraged his followers. His 'sign' turned out to be a huge misunderstanding, with the Almighty helping the other side. Those rebels who were not cut down, stabbed or trampled by warhorses in the bloody fracas later died by the executioner's sword or on the gallows.

Shortly before the conclusive combat Müntzer, who since his tirade against his rulers at Schloss Allstedt had been refused any form of reconciliation, sent a letter "*To brother Albrecht von Mansfeld, written for his conversion*", saying, "*If you will acknowledge Daniel 7[:27], according to which God has given power to the common man, and if you are willing to appear before us and retract your stance, then we will gladly accommodate you and treat us as our common brother. But if you do not, then we will [...] fight against you as against an arch-enemy of the Christian faith: that is for sure.*"

Martin Luther of course also knew of the despotism and tyranny of the princes and of the terrible plight of the peasants. He thus initially justified their rebellion, writing "*It is no wonder they revolt – it is only their wretched situation that prevents them from raging more terribly.*" However, it wasn't long before he could no longer approve of their dreadful acts of violence, prompted by their sense of hopelessness and blind anger. This is important if we are to understand why he wrote his treatise *Against the Robbing and Murdering Hordes of Peasants.*

The gift of life

The medieval history of Schmalkalden was largely written by the House of Henneberg. As opposed to the territorial limitations of his estates in Schleusingen the diplomatic skills of Count Berthold VII (1284–1340) were many and great. He thus made himself useful to no less than three kings, extracting the utmost profit from their thankful rewards. He was not only made a prince but also received control of Schmalkalden, the ruling of which the Hennebergs had to share with the landgraves of Hesse just a few decades later in 1360. This led to a situation which was extremely rare for the Reformation. While Philipp of Hesse chose Schmalkalden as the seat of a coalition against the Catholics and the emperor, known to history as the League of Schmalkalden, the dynasty of Henneberg stuck most vehemently to the old Catholic ways.

Of the ten meetings held by the Protestants at Schloss Wallrabs, now the Wilhelmsburg, those in February and March of 1537 were the most important. The Great Convention was attended by 28 princes, the mayors of 22 cities of the

Holy Roman Empire, the emperor's vice chancellor and the papal nuncio, among others. Luther had prepared a paper which was passed during the proceedings as the *Schmalkald Articles* yet was unable to personally attend as he lay ill in bed. His urethra was blocked by a stone which even the doctor brought in from Erfurt was unable to remove. For nine days Luther was unable to pass water. His body swelled up like a barrel and the pain he had to bear grew increasingly worse. Luther was then saved by one of the godly interventions he himself viewed with great scepticism. While being transported through the Thuringian Forest in deference to his request to die in the Electorate of Saxony, the carriage and the patient were so thoroughly rocked and shaken that the urinary calculus decided to exit Luther's body before his soul did.

Theatrical machinations in Gotha

Duke Ernst I (1601–1675), known as The Pious, could also have been called The Thrifty. When four candles were placed next to his bed when travelling, there were two too many. The cow he gave his wife for her birthday – she bore him 18 children – wasn't allowed to cost more than five florins. One of his mottoes was "Richness comes not from taking richly but from giving poorly". His economy had limitations, however. His palatial residence of Friedenstein (one of the largest palaces in Germany) was one such example, where absolutely nothing was left to be desired. He also earned himself much credit with his system of Protestant schools. He not only had children from the age of five to thirteen taught here but also examined the (religious) knowledge of their parents. This gave rise to the saying *"Ein gothaischer Bauer hat zehnmal mehr Mores / als anderswo Adlige und Doctores! "*, which roughly translates as *"Ten times more manners have peasants from Gotha / Than elsewhere the nobles and many a doctor!"*

Ignoring his disgraceful role on the stage of world politics – he sold children as soldiers to war-waging parties in countries far and wide – the duke's son Friedrich loved the arts above all else. He thus had a theatre built in the west tower of his palace. The first major performance – of the lyrical drama *The Rape of Proserpine* – was staged in honour of his wife Christine's birthday in 1683. The play was also a demonstration of what contemporary theatrical machinery was capable of. While Ceres, Venus and Mercury flew through the air, Pluto crawled up from the depths in order to make a grab for Proserpina. The din of the flying machines and scenery wagons must have been deafening.

Schmalkalden, which for
about six centuries
belonged not to Thuringia
but to Hesse, represents
a major chapter in the
history of the German
Reformation. One half-
timbered medieval house
after another adorns its
centre.

The baroque theatre, still used for productions, bears the name of Conrad Ekhof who played here with his company in the 1770s. The famous principal was an early and rather unexpected boon to the history of German theatre. Of decidedly unremarkable appearance – Heinrich AO Reichard once described him as a *"small, unassuming man [...] with an offensive tongue, with [...] feet that turned inwards, supported by a type of crutch and waddling along bent and bowed"* – once on stage he underwent an incredible transformation, his talents directing attention away from his bowed form.

The sorrows of young Bach

On August 9, 1703, Johann Sebastian Bach arrived in Arnstadt. His responsibilities included playing the organ and also conducting the school choir. And here there were problems. His attitude to teaching even then was that of a necessary evil. He also lacked patience in dealing with young people who were glad of the chance to earn a little money by singing. Bach had very different ideas. The stage was thus set for conflict. Bach publically referred to his pupil Geyersbach as a "nanny-goat bassoonist"; in return, the young man called his teacher a "miserable cur" and went for him with a stick. Bach then drew his dagger and the two had to be forcibly separated. This was in the summer of 1705.

In October Bach took four weeks' holiday in order to visit the great Dieterich Buxtehude in Lübeck. The latter was already 70 years old and the prospect of becoming his successor was extremely enticing to the young composer. Bach thus sought the company of the master for as long as possible – and four weeks turned into four months. It was thus no wonder that there was a storm brewing in Arnstadt. On his return the consistory demanded an explanation and an apology for his long absence without leave – both of which Bach refused to give. His behaviour was the last straw. The accusations against him were many: he was unable to 'comport' himself with his choir; the manner in which he dealt with church services was anything other than satisfactory; he had *"made so many wonderful variations in the choral, mixing in many strange notes, that the congregation was confounded by them"*. And the previous Sunday he had been "*in the wine cellar during the sermon*". He should dwell upon these and many other things which disturbed both the consistory and the parish at large and affect to counteract the impression that he be "incorrigible" and unable to better himself. Despite this dusting down Bach remained in Arnstadt until 1707 when he moved to Mühlhausen.

The Henrys of Reuß

Of all the German royal houses that of the Reuß dynasty seems to have been most disposed towards separation and the forming of collateral lines. After having split up one of their royal capitals, it wouldn't be inaccurate to assume that they would have carried on dividing until there was nothing left of them – had the emperor not forbidden them to do so in 1681. They were subsequently the subject of much ridicule by the rest of the empire. Heinrich Heine compared the state of the House of Reuß to that of Farther Pomerania. In Karl Gutzkov's play *Zopf und Schwert* or Plait and Sword from 1844 a Prussian princess claims she would rather be a member of the Reuß-Greiz-Schleiz and Lobenstein dynasty that marry someone she didn't love. On October 21, 1878, Heinrich XXII of Reuß (of the Elder Line) seized the chance to revenge the humiliation his extended family had suffered in being the only member of parliament to not condone Bismarck's law "against the generally dangerous endeavours of the Socialists" – causing Prussia to break off diplomatic relations. The dynasty of Reuß were originally vogts of the Vogtland, the imperial estates in the vague vicinity of Gera. They were later made princes. To this very day all male heirs are named after their founding father Heinrich or Henry of Gleißberg (c.1040 – c.1120). A local rhyme scorned the self-importance of the family and their modest holdings, claiming "*Greiz, Schleiz, Lobenstein / Sind drei kleine Nester, / Greiz, das ist die Residenz / Zeulenroda die Schwester. / Und sind die beiden noch so klein, / Lobenstein könnt' grösser sein*" or "*Greiz, Schleiz, Lobenstein / Are very easy to miss here / Greiz is the royal capital / And Zeulenroda the sister. / And though the two be very small, / Lobenstein is no greater at all.*" – The two remaining territories of Hirschberg and Ebersdorf were obviously so tiny as to not deserve a mention...

As a result of the aforementioned divisions Greiz or the "pearl of the Vogtland" now has two regal palaces, with a magnificent park along the banks of the River Elster. Originally laid out in the formal French style, it has since been informally landscaped à la Capability Brown. The early neoclassical palace has a unique collection of copper engravings which

was collated by two English princesses, both daughters of King George III. One of them, Elisabeth, married into the House of Hesse-Nassau. Her legacy included the famous collection which was brought to the little town of Greiz.

(Almost) forgotten: Joseph Meyer

On December 4, 1828, Joseph Meyer (1796–1856) decided to make the Brunnquellsches Haus in Hildburghausen his new Bibliographical Institute which, founded two years previously in Gotha, he had feared was doomed. Having to start again was not new to him; in his twenties he had earned spectacular sums of money on the London stock exchange – and gambled it all away. Mayer saw the book as an item of sale, destroying its elitist reputation and turning it into a mass product. His first brilliant idea was his Miniature Library of German Classics, providing good literature at a price most people could afford – although in doing so he disregarded the interests of established publishers, booksellers and even authors. He was tried at court for being a "stealer of privileges" where neither his defence of possessing a "philanthropic attitude" nor his protestations of being on a "mission for civilisation" were able to help him. His printing house was shut down and he was banished from the land.

His adversaries rejoiced – but too soon. Meyer tried again in Hildburghausen and this time did things better. He added ancient texts to his range of German classics, plus a Historical Library, a "people's library for nature-lovers", various editions of the Bible, a universal work of reference in twelve languages for 80,000 subscribers and many other titles. The original edition personally edited by Joseph Meyer (1839–1855) amounted to 52 large-format volumes; a more manageable size issued 50 years later still numbered 15 tomes. Meyer as a bookseller was just as imaginative as he was as a printer. By introducing book subscription to Germany he committed readers to his editions. The idea of selling books door to door – like shoe cream, shoelaces and garters – was even more successful. These salesmen called themselves travelling booksellers or peddlers and later became synonymous with more trivial types of literature. In 1850 Meyer spoke of having distributed 25 million volumes across the world. Not bad for someone once hauled before the courts …

Schifflersgrund Museum on the border of Thuringia and Hesse, opened in 1991, reminds us of the decades when Germany was split by the East/West divide. These sculptures by Sebastian Seiffert commemorate the 26 people who died here.

A warm welcome

There may be plenty of books around on Thuringia but these can never replace the impressions made in real life. Getting there is much easier now the new A71 and A73 motorways have been built through the Thuringian Forest. The winter resort of Oberhof has also been made much more attractive. Its annual world cup events are something of a giant party, with both locals and visitors in high spirits. The Sommergewinn in Eisenach is another Thuringian jollity not to be missed and one of Germany's oldest and biggest to boot. Others include the onion market in Weimar on the second weekend in October and the Christmas bauble market in Lauscha on the first and second Sundays in Advent. Rudolstadt is also not to be missed in the summer if you fancy visiting Germany's biggest festival of folk, roots and world music.

And where there are festivities, there are sausages. Thuringia is famous for them and together with the dumpling or *Kloß* its *Thüringer Rostbratwürste* top the list of local dishes. Luckily there's also plenty of opportunity to work off the collateral damage of too many of these delicacies – by hiking in the Thüringer Wald or Thuringian Forest, for example. Or cycling. Or paragliding, hang gliding and the like. Or being active in or on the water. One of the most frequented resorts for the latter is the Hohenwarte Reservoir, part of the long cascade of the River Saale and a perfect place to swim, relax – and maybe eat another sausage or two...

Page 22/23:
It was in this Renaissance abode, the southernmost of the three Dornburg palaces, that Goethe spent an entire summer busy writing following the death of his friend Carl August, the duke of Weimar.

Page 24/25:
It sometimes snows as early as October in the Thuringian Forest, whose white cloak is usually a fixed feature from November to April.

26 Tote an der Grenze
Hessen / Thüringen

Sie wollten von
Deutschland nach Deutschland

From the state capital to the Goldene Aue

The old fish market in Erfurt. The Roman warrior on his lofty pedestal has grand views wherever he looks, with wonderful Renaissance houses to the left and the neo-Gothic town hall on the right.

Throughout its long history Erfurt on the southern edge of the Thuringian Basin has belonged to heathens and Christians, the Electorate of Mainz and the Electorate of Saxony, Sweden, France and Prussia – but rarely to itself. Despite its former power and significance, it was never a free city of the Holy Roman Empire. When in 1920 various small states joined together to form Thuringia Erfurt was left out, only to be included at the end of the Second World War. It seems incredible that Erfurt was the capital of the federal state for just four years before the Berlin Wall came down.

Not far from Erfurt are two other destinations of great appeal. One is Eisenach with the magnificent Wartburg and the other Gotha, which has one of the most impressive art collections in what was formerly East Germany stored at Schloss Friedenstein. Mühlhausen boasts a splendid medieval centre which after decades of neglect has now been restored in a truly exemplary fashion.

North of the flat basin the land slowly begins to rise with the hills of the Eichsfeld and the Dün, Hainleite, Schmücke and Finne, miniature mountains that barely reach the 500-metre or 1,600-foot mark. Kyffhäuser Mountain in the area known as the Goldene Aue is no exception yet it is still extremely popular as it is allegedly the place where Emperor Friedrich Barbarossa lies sleeping within. At the end of the 19th century he suddenly became visible on the summit – chiselled in stone, together with Emperor Wilhelm I. If you wish to raise a glass to the two deceased rulers, a local *Korn* from Nordhausen is recommended, distilled – as the name would suggest – in Thuringia's northernmost city.

Right:
The Krämerbrücke across the Breitstrom, a side arm of the River Gera, seen from the north. The original wooden bridge was first mentioned in 1117, with the stone version dating back to 1325.

Below:
The three-storey, half-timbered houses on the wide Krämerbrücke were built following a fierce fire in 1472. Of the 62 originally erected, only 32 still stand.

When the first wooden bridge was put up about 900 years ago, it was soon lined with stalls selling all kinds of wares. These modern-day boutiques on the Krämerbrücke continue this tradition.

Above:
St Severi, an early Gothic hall church with a nave and four aisles, was begun at the end of the 13th century and finished in the mid 1300s. The magnificent vaulting took 100 years longer to complete.

Right:
The ornate northwest entrance to the cathedral with its foolish and wise maidens Ecclesia and Synagoga and, in the tympanum, the Holy Trinity, dates back to the 13th century.

Right page:
View of the high Gothic choir of the cathedral, built between 1349 and 1372.

30

Right:
Modern fountain on Anger, the main square in the state capital of Thuringia. In the southeast of the old town, the square was first mentioned in 1196.

Far right:
The Luther monument on Anger shows the Reformer with a Bible open in his hands. Martin Luther lived in Erfurt between 1501 and 1508, first as a student and later as a monk.

Buildings from several different epochs line Anger square. The main post office with its tower is from the late 19th century, its façade a mixture of sandstone, clinker brick and terracotta. Angereck on the left of the photo is a modern edifice from the year 2000.

These fighting boys on the fountain on Wenigemarkt are by sculptor Heinrich Apel from Magdeburg. The little market square is at the eastern end of the Krämerbrücke.

So that the many visitors to the Krämerbrücke need not go hungry or thirsty, Wenigemarkt next door has plenty of catering outlets. This charming square was first mentioned in 1217.

Erfurt doors I. A door is like a face. It not only tells us when the house behind it was erected but is also a manifestation of the wealth and tastes of its owners and of the skill of the builders, craftsmen and artists who contributed to its makeup. The Haus zum Roten Ochsen on Fischmarkt (above) sports an ox, the Muses and the Ancient gods of the planets. The Haus zum Stockfisch (right) is also Renaissance; Haus Dacherröden is on the Angerbrunnen (far right).

HAUS ZUM SONNEBORN

Erfurt doors II. They can be playful or severe, elaborate and colourful or simple and reserved in their design. Haus zum Sonneborn (far left) is now Erfurt's registry office. The portals on Anger are no less splendid (left) and on Domplatz the Renaissance Haus zur Hohen Lilie once accommodated such illustrious guests as Martin Luther, Philipp Melanchthon and Swedish King Gustav Adolf II.

"If someone had taught me then what I now believe and teach through the grace of God, I would have torn him apart with my teeth", Luther once said of his time as a monk in Erfurt's Augustinian monastery which was built in 1277.

Thuringia's state chancellery is based in a patrician house from 1640 which was where the electorate of Mainz held office from 1720 onwards. The baroque façade was planned by Maximilian von Welsch.

Right page:
egapark Erfurt is both a garden show and a recreation ground. The area surrounding the ruined Cyriaksburg citadel was turned into a park in the 1920s and used for big international garden exhibitions during the days of the GDR.

Below:
Entrusted with difficult diplomatic quests by the king and the nobility and adored by the ladies, Count Gustav Adolf von Gotter

(1692–1762) turned the old manor of Molsdorf into a glorious venue in which to indulge in the delights of the Rococo period.

Top right:
Veste Wachsenburg goes back to the 10th century and the imperial abbey of Hersfeld which owned many estates near Arnstadt.

Centre right:
In the 12th and 13th centuries the fortress of Wachsenburg changed hands between the Welfs and the Staufer and later between the Schwarzburgs and Apel von Vitzthum, also known as the 'fire chief' of Thuringia. The castle is now a hotel and museum.

Bottom right:
Shepherd near Mühlberg, one of the oldest towns in Thuringia. It was first mentioned on May 1, 704, in a deed of gift from Duke Hedan II of Thuringia to Bishop Willibrord of Utrecht.

Left page:
The Renaissance town hall on Hauptmarkt in Gotha was originally a department store, erected between 1567 and 1577 by master builders Caspar Mans, Christoph Götze and Nicolaus Rausche.

What was the natural history museum in Gotha will be an art gallery once it has been converted. The plant and animal exhibits will find a new home in Schloss Friedenstein.

Schloss Friedrichsthal east of Schloss Friedenstein in Gotha goes back to the beginning of the 18th century. It was constructed by director of works Wolf Cristoph Zorn von Plobsheim. The man who both commissioned and named the palace was Duke Friedrich II of Saxe-Gotha-Altenburg.

Left page:
View of Hauptmarkt in Gotha from Schlossberg or the castle mound. In the background is the Margarethenkirche, built in the 15th century on Roman foundations.

The orangery in Gotha, once the duke's kitchen garden, is heralded as one of the largest and most beautiful baroque parks of its kind in the whole of Germany.

The vast edifice of Schloss Friedenstein in Gotha, built to replace the castle of Grimmenstein which was razed to the ground in 1567, dates back to Duke Ernst the Pious (1601–1675).

43

Small photos, right:
The collections housed in Schloss Friedenstein are among the most extensive and significant in what used to be East Germany. They include a gallery of paintings, with the famous Gotha Lovers, a chamber of copper engravings, a collection of antiquities and a coin museum. Various rooms in the ducal residence are also open to the public.

Left page:
The town hall in Eisenach, the core of which is late Gothic, goes back to 1508. Half a century later it was refurbished in the Renaissance style and later completely rebuilt following the great fire of 1636.

Below:
The Nikolaikirche in Eisenach, thought to have been erected in the last quarter of the 12th century, is an aisled Roman basilica. Up until the Reformation it served as the parish church to a Benedictine convent.

Above:
The Bach House in Eisenach gives visitors an impression of what life was like for a middle-class family during Bach's lifetime. A permanent exhibition documents the various stages in the great composer's life. There are also historic instruments on display; talks and concerts are also held here.

Right:
The statue of Bach in Eisenach, designed by Adolf von Donndorf (1835–1916) of Weimar, was unveiled in 1884 and is now outside the Bach House.

Page 50/51:
The Romanesque great
hall is the oldest part of
Wartburg Castle. The two
lower storeys originated
between 1190 and 1220,
with the top floor added
in c. 1350.

Left:
Adolf von Donndorf also
fashioned the bronze
statue of Luther in 1895
that stands on Karlsplatz
in Eisenach.

Below:
The late 15th-century
Cottasches Haus (a Luther
house), one of the oldest
and prettiest town resi-
dences in Eisenach, was
rebuilt after being destroyed
during the Second World
War. It's said that Luther
lived here while he was a
Latin scholar (1498–1501).

WARTBURG CASTLE – ARENA OF GERMANY HISTORY

I am as if possessed with the life of Saint Elisabeth; what a time! Everything has been designed but one can only start thinking of execution next year. Throughout the summer I wish to see what useful things I might find in Eisenach and Marburg", wrote Moritz von Schwind in the middle of the 19th century. He had been commissioned by the grand duke of Weimar with the artistic embellishment of the Wartburg, recently awakened from its deep slumber. Among other works for the castle the famous Romantic master painted six frescoes depicting important stations in the life of this unusual lady. One of these was the miracle of the rose; when her husband pulled back Elisabeth's cloak to see what was hidden underneath it, God turned the food she had been secretly been taking to the poor and sick into roses.

The landgravine of Thuringia is one of the great programmatic female figures of the Christian West. Those who speak of compassion, self-sacrifice and humility must first look to Elisabeth. In 1211, at the age of four, the daughter of king of Hungary Andrew II and his wife Gertrud of Merania was sent to Eisenach. By the time she was eighteen she had given birth to three children and died when just twenty-four. Among the saintly lady's great admirers was Franz Liszt who dedicated an oratorio to her in 1867 when the Wartburg was officially reopened. Theodor Fontane, also in Eisenach during this period, fled the celebrations; the vast throng was simply too much for him. His commentary was accordingly caustic: *"Everybody who held with the triumvirate of Liszt, Wagner and Bülow was there: virtuosi with a general's swagger, young genii with long and female altos with short hair – there was nothing lacking. In the end the abbot Liszt appeared in person ..."*

War and peace

Before the arrival of Elisabeth Walther von der Vogelweide, Wolfram von Eschenbach, Reinmar der Alte, Heinrich von Ofterdingen, Biterolf and Heinrich von Risbach are thought to have convened at the Wartburg for the legendary Sängerkrieg or contest of the minstrels. The object of the exercise wasn't to select the best poet and performer but the one who best flattered the landgrave. Heinrich von Ofterdingen obviously couldn't or didn't want to display the required amount of subservient enthusiasm; as he instead sang the praises of his Austrian patron, he ended up in last place – which meant

death for the rebellious minnesinger. Thank goodness, then, that at just the right moment the sorcerer Klingsor whizzed over from Hungary – on a cloud – to rescue the foolish Ofterdingen.

Scholars are still not agreed as to when or even if this spectacle actually took place. It is a known fact that both Walther von der Vogelweide and Wolfram von Eschenbach spent time at the Wartburg. The presence of Heinrich von Risbach and Biterolf is also assured, as they were members of the landgrave's court.

Three centuries later on being excommunicated by the pope Martin Luther sought asylum at the castle. Disguised as Junker Jörg (the Knight George), in 1521/22 he began translating the New Testament from Greek into German. His justified his reasons for doing so thus: *"We must not [...] ask the Latin letters how to speak German: but we must ask the mother in the home, the children on the street, the common man in the market place, how this is done, their lips we must watch to see how they speak, and then we must translate accordingly. Then they will understand us and notice that we are talking German with them"* Luther wasn't just a great thinker but also an extremely talented neologist. Many of his quotes and sayings have thus become general property.

Another major event to take place at Wartburg Castle was the mass convention of Germany's student fraternities in 1817. After Luther had pleaded for the "freedom of the Christian man" 300 years before, these young people, many of whom had fought in the wars of liberation against Napoleon, now argued, *"Those who may bleed for the Fatherland may also speak of how they might best serve it in times of peace!"*

Left:
Sorcerer Klingsor from Hungary is said to have climbed the keep of the Wartburg and predicted the birth of Saint Elisabeth by reading the stars ...

Above:
Legend has it that the Wartburg dates back to Count Ludwig the Jumper (1042–1123) who on seeing the mountain is said to have uttered the words: "Wait, mountain, for you shall become my castle".

Small photos, right:
Once Wartburg Castle had lost its strategic importance and its attraction as a place of residence, it fell into ruin. This was at the end of the 16th century. The man who later initiated its reconstruction was none other than Johann Wolfgang von Goethe.

Below:
Eisenach. The town evolved from three small market villages and was first mentioned in c. 1180. From the end of the 12th century to 1406 it was the seat of the landgraves of Thuringia. Eisenach now has a population of about 42,000.

Top right:
*The Burschenschafts-
denkmal erected on the
Göpelskuppe above
Eisenach between 1900*

*and 1902 from plans by
Wilhelm Kreis commemo-
rates the members of
student fraternities who
fought for the Fatherland.*

Bottom right:
*Countryside north of
Eisenach. The highland
plateau stretches as far
as the Hainich, a huge
forested upland ridge
whose highest point
almost hits the 500-metre
mark (1,640 feet).*

Right:
The market church of St Boniface rises tall above the historic old town of Bad Langensalza. The foundation stone was laid in 1395, the vaulting completed in 1521. Six decades later the steeple was given its Renaissance top.

Far right:
The town hall fountain in Bad Langensalza goes back to 1582. The two lions with their coats of arms denote Saxony (the black lion) and Thuringia (the red-and-silver striped lion).

Friederikenschlösschen in Bad Langensalza, erected in the mid 18th century, is now the tourist information centre and a venue for local events. It dates back to Dowager Duchess Friederike von Sachsen-Weißenfels.

Far left:
Mühlhausen is rich in historical buildings. The old free imperial city was also a member of the Hanseatic League and positively boomed in the 14th and 15th centuries.

Left:
When Untermarkt in Mühlhausen was redesigned, its fountain was removed. Only these statues of three children playing have remained.

Far left:
The Divi-Blasii Church in Mühlhausen, where Johann Sebastian Bach worked from June 15, 1707, to June 25, 1708, was given its present guise in the 13th and 14th centuries. If you come here at the right time of the day, you can see the rose window in the north transept aglow with celestial light.

Left:
Marienkirche in Mühlhausen was built on the site of a Roman church between 1317 and 1380. The enormous place of worship, which contains marvellous Gothic winged altarpieces and stone carvings, has been used as a museum since 1975.

Left page:
Schifflersgrund Museum, opened in 1991 on the border between Thuringia and Hesse, was the first of its kind in Germany and documents a Germany divided into political East and West.

On May 14, 2009, a treetop trail was opened in the Hainich National Park which is the largest consolidated area of deciduous forest in Germany. You can wander among the trees here along two giant suspended loops.

A gigantic monument was erected on the site of the old imperial castle of Kyffhausen between 1891 and 1896 which linked Kaiser Wilhelm I to the legend that Emperor Barbarossa will one day return.

Page 60/61:
Heldrungen was built in the 13th century as a Romanesque moated castle. It later fell to the counts of Mansfeld. After the royal troops had defeated the rebellious peasants on May 15, 1525, their leader Thomas Müntzer was imprisoned in the castle and tortured.

59

Right:
The historic town hall in Nordhausen, once an imperial free city and Hanseatic town, took on its present form in c. 1610. The statue of Roland on the corner of the Renaissance building stands for the confidence and power of its local citizens.

Far right:
Nordhausen between the Hainleite and Unterharz goes back 1,000 years. Up until 1802 it was a free city of the Holy Roman Empire.

Below:
Until the end of the Second World War Nordhausen was a major site of production for chewing tobacco. This is documented at the tobacco store (two half-timbered barns) that is part of Nordhausen's museum of trading and industrial history and archaeology.

Above:
Nordhausen has been making its famous Korn schnapps for 500 years, with the traditional Echter Nordhäuser distillery in operation for the last 100. The products on sale here are many and can be savoured (if not all at once) at the café.

Left and far left:
The oldest parts of the cathedral in Nordhausen, dating back to the Romanesque period, are the bases of the east towers and the crypt with its three aisles. The early Gothic choir was added in c. 1250. The flat roof was replaced by a stellar vault in the 16th century.

From Weimar to Altenburg

Looking over Grand Duke Carl August's shoulder you can see the oldest parts of the palace in Weimar: the tower and what is know as the Bastille. The statue was created by Adolf von Donndorf.

Weimar first featured in the history of German art and intellectualism when Lucas Cranach the Elder moved to the city in 1552, one year before his death. In 1617 the Fruchtbringende Gesellschaft or Societas fructifera was founded at the palace, whose members included the dukes of Weimar and Köthen and also famous poets such as Martin Opitz, Andreas Gryphius and Friedrich von Logau. They strived to maintain "our mother tongue in its basic form and proper meaning without the intervention of unfamiliar foreign words" – both now and then a seemingly endless task.

Jena was frequently visited by Goethe. He introduced natural scientists of renown to the university where he worked on experiments with his esteemed colleagues. The discovery of the human intermaxillary bone is one result of his time spent in Jena, his *Theory of Colours* another. At the climax of the Industrial Revolution Fate brought together three more great minds in Jena. One was Carl Zeiss who in 1846 opened a mechanics workshop, the second Ernst Abbe who applied his revolutionary notions on refraction to the lens. Chemist Otto Schott ensured that the new lenses had the required quality; he was the only one of the three whose small company later become an international concern.

Altenburg is one of the oldest cities in the federal state. The castle, first mentioned in 976, was erected to guard both the recently conquered Pleißegau and the young market town. The best-known section of the castle museum is that dedicated to the history of playing cards. Altenburg is namely where the popular German card game Skat was invented. Those who prefer more ethereal pleasures will find these here too on the wonderful tableaux of the Italian Gothic and Early Renaissance on display at Lindenau Museum.

"The town is only small and besides the ducal palace there are no further buildings of any size", wrote Russian poet Nikolai Karamsin on visiting Weimar in 1789. What he saw was the fourth regal residence, built after fire had consumed the first three. It was only completed ten years after his visit.

Weimar's neo-Gothic
Rathaus from 1842 stands
on the west side of the
market square on the site
of the old council building.
The plans were drawn up
by Heinrich Heß.

The Rotes Schloss dates
back to 1574. Initially a
residence for royal
widows, at the beginning
of the 18th century the
court orchestra moved in.
It later housed the Free
School of Drawing, which
Goethe helped found, and
the ministry of finance.

Left page:
The Cranachhaus on Weimar's market place was erected by local architect Nikolaus Gromann between 1547 and 1549. Famous painter Lucas Cranach lived here from September 26, 1552, up until his death on October 16, 1553.

Far left:
Fried sausage and dumplings are probably the best known items on the menu in Thuringia – and there's an enormous range to choose from. This elderly waitress is advertising the Scharfe Ecke restaurant.

Left:
Neptunbrunnen is the oldest fountain in Weimar. When it was erected at the end of the 16th century it first bore a stone lion, the city's heraldic animal. The statue of Neptune made by royal sculptor Martin Gottlieb Klauer replaced the big cat in 1774.

Left:
The Zum Zwiebel restaurant on Teichgasse in Weimar not only serves onion soup and onion flan but also many other local specialities, such as barbecued Rostbrätel pork steak, spicy braised beef and the obligatory Thuringian dumplings fried in bacon.

Page 70/71:
The Stadtkirche is inextricably linked to Johann Gottfried Herder, after whom it is named. The great writer and philosopher was head pastor and general superintendent here for 26 years.

69

Grand Duke Carl August by Adolf Donndorf, seen from the other side. To the right is a section of the old royal palace, now the music conservatoire named after Franz Liszt, with the Herzogin Anna Amalia Bibliothek on the left.

Travelling Weimar as Goethe may once have done, with the writer's house in the background. The simple, two-storey baroque edifice from 1709 was where Goethe lived and worked for 47 years. Large sections of the collections dedicated to art and science he collated "with planning and deliberation" have found a home here.

The west top storey of this baroque building erected by Anton Georg Hauptmann in 1770 was where Charlotte von Stein lived, Goethe's close friend and confidante. This clever woman with her great appreciation of the arts was so important to Goethe during the first ten years he was in Weimar that he wrote her around 1,700 letters, some extremely long.

This classic bus, a replica Talbot from 1925, takes visitors on tours of Weimar. The fourth-largest city in Thuringia is not just famous for its Classical poets; it was also once home to the Bauhaus.

Right:
The neoclassical Großes Haus is one of the venues of the German National Theatre and Weimar's state orchestra. The famous statue of Goethe and Schiller outside it from 1857 is the work of Ernst Rietschel.

Far right:
The Bauhaus Museum. The multifaceted Belgian artist Henry van de Velde set up a school of applied arts here in 1905/06 which Walter Gropius merged with the school of painting and sculpture to form the Bauhaus in 1919.

Below:
The Goethehaus on Frauenplan lit up at night. The name of the square comes from a chapel dedicated to Our Blessed Lady which disappeared at the beginning of the 16th century. The fountain dates back to 1822.

Above:
Buchenwald was a concentration camp on Ettersberg in Weimar where tens of thousands of people were systematically murdered. This famous group of figures commemorating the victims is by Fritz Cremer.

Left:
Café-restaurant Frauentor on Schillerstraße. When the poet acquired his house it was on the edge of town, "surrounded on all sides by gardens and parks. The advantages of a city dwelling were married with the pleasantries of a garden house" (Fritz Kühnlenz).

WEIMAR'S FAMOUS TEMPLES OF THE MUSES

It is thanks to the initiative of perceptive arts patron Duchess Anna Amalia and the contributions of Goethe, Schiller, Herder, Wieland and others that the Greek Muses Clio, Euterpe, Thalia, Melpomene, Terpischore, Erato, Polyhymnia, Urania and Calliope have comfortably ensconced themselves in so many places in and around Weimar. The weekly round table held at the Wittumspalais, to whence the young widow retired after the great palace fire of 1774, attracted famous personages from various walks of life. It is remarkable that under certain conditions members of the public were also allowed to witness these intellectual disputes. A patched skirt or darned stocking were no grounds for exclusion; lack of cleanliness was, however. In the exhibition halls of the present Duchess Anna Amalia Library Christoph Martin Wieland, the man who acted as a go-between for the duchess and the Muses, is especially revered. Both a master of the pen and a true connoisseur of life, Wieland was an expert on Ancient Greek and Roman philosophy and literature and the characters these featured – with a particular fondness for the erotic.

Tiefurt, Belvedere and Ettersburg

"In honour of the sublime, enjoyment of the beautiful, the creating of good" is how Goethe once described the spirit of the palace and park of Tiefurt. At Anna Amalia's summer residence beyond the city gates the restrictions of court protocol and etiquette could be escaped for a least a short while. The spirits of the great and the good who once nurtured their utopia and ideals here are omnipresent. A pyramid featuring a butterfly, the symbol of genius, reminds us of Herder. A bust designed by Johann Gottfried Schadow marks Wieland's favourite spot on the River Ilm. An allegorical statue of Cupid by Martin Gottlieb Klauer, who feeds a nightingale with the point of his arrow and poisons it, pays homage to the beautiful actress Corona Schröter. The most famous and impressive monument is the temple of friendship, with carefully planted flowers, lawns and trees forming a natural wreath of honour. A journal published in an edition of 47 between 1781 and 1784, with just eleven handwritten copies of each issue, included contributions by almost everyone who was anyone at Tiefurt. It also contained Goethe's much quoted adage "Noble be man, helpful and good!"

The baroque palace of Belvedere dates back to Duke Ernst August. Built as a lodge for pheasant hunting between 1724 and 1732 by Johann Adolph Richter und Gottfried Heinrich Krohne a riding hall, ballroom, kennels, menagerie, orangery and park were gradually added. During a veritable garden revolution some of the palace walls were torn down and the park was completely redesigned, the formal French symmetry replaced by informal 'English' landscaping. Incidentally, as mentioned by Goethe in his poem *Die Lustigen von Weimar* (The Merry Folk of Weimar), for some reason Thursday was the day to visit Belvedere ...

Ettersburg, the third temple of the Muses out in the country, was not only built by the same architects but was also used by the same successor. The amateur dramatic productions put on by Anna Amalia in her palace and on her stage were the talk of the town. Goethe wrote the plays and adapted them. The court performed tales such as *Jahrmarktsfest zu Plundersweilern* (Plundersweiler Fair), *Die Vögel* (The Birds) and *Iphigenia*. Great literature was written here: this is where Goethe worked on *Tasso* and Schiller on *Maria Stuart*. After finishing the first four acts Schiller felt in need of "poetic solitude" which he found in Ettersburg from May 23 to June 2, 1800. Less than two weeks later the drama of the fated Mary Queen of Scots was premiered at the court theatre.

Left:
When in September 2004 angry flames consumed the library of Duchess Anna Amalia it seemed incredible that within just three years it would rise from the ashes more glorious than ever before.

Above:
Schloss Belvedere, built between 1724 and 1732, is now a museum of the Rococo period.

Small photos, right, from top to bottom: Under Duchess Anna Amalia the Wittumspalais became one of the intellectual centres of Weimar.

What would Weimar be without Goethe? No other name is as strongly associated with Weimar as his.

The temple of friendship in the park of Schloss Tiefurt with the figure of Polyhymnia, the Muse of song.

The gardens of Schloss Belvedere were partly landscaped by Prince Pückler-Muskau.

77

Above:
Schloss Belvedere is a few miles from the centre of Weimar. The dominant middle section is topped by a small viewing tower.

Right:
The bronze statue of Herder from 1850 is outside the church where the leading theoretician of the Sturm und Drang period and pioneer of German Classicism worked for many years.

Far right:
The Russian Orthodox church in Weimar's Historischer Friedhof was erected in 1860 as a chapel of rest for Grand Duchess Maria Pavlovna (1786–1859), the wife of Grand Duke Carl Friedrich.

Above:
Goethe's garden house.
On May 17, 1776, Goethe
wrote to Countess Stolberg:
"I have a pretty little
garden outside the gates
on the beautiful meadows
of the Ilm; there's an old
house in it I'm going to
have repaired…"

Left:
When Grand Duke Carl
August voiced his desire
for a permanent summer
residence on the River Ilm,
Goethe advised: "Act as
if you were building for
yourself; our needs were
always similar". The result
was the Römisches Haus,
a neo-Roman villa built in
1791–97.

Below:
Avenue near the little town of Apolda, famous for its bell foundries, on the southeastern edge of the Thuringian Basin which runs into the Muschelkalk formation of the Ilm-Saale Plateau here.

Top right:
The most southerly of the three famous castles of Dirnburg erected in 1539 by Volrad von Watzdorf is from the Renaissance period.

An inscription on one of the window frames reads: "Goethe stayed here from July 7 to September 12 in 1828 ", written by the great poet himself.

Centre and bottom right: *In many of its features the baroque French garden surrounding the Rococo palace of Dornburg echoes the décor of the interior.*

The lines are generously curved, with spirals of box, arches of greenery and a diffusion of colour paying homage to the copious ornamentation of the age.

Above:
At 85 x 60 metres or ca. 280 x 200 feet, the market place in Jena is one of the largest yet most compact in Thuringia. It has a Gothic Rathaus or town hall and a monument to Johann Friedrich I, founder of the University of Jena.

Right:
Cafés and restaurants line Wagnergasse in Jena like a string of pearls. As soon as spring starts and the Muschelkalk slopes begin to warm the valley of the River Saale, bistro tables and chairs appear on the pavements.

Left:
The Zeiss Planetarium is one of the most frequented sights in Jena. The building with its colonnaded entrance was built in 1925/26. The dome spans 25 metres or 82 feet.

Page 84/85:
View of Jena from JenTower. This centre of science and education in the valley of the Saale, with its long tradition of scholarship and research, now has ca. 105,000 inhabitants, with over 2,000 of them students at Jena's Friedrich Schiller University.

Far left:
The enormous Goethe Galerie, a spectacular shopping and amusement centre, was erected in just 27 months on the site of the old Carl Zeiss factory. This successful synthesis of old and new was awarded a real-estate Oscar in Cannes in 1997.

Left:
View along Wagnergasse of the JenTower, 133 metres or 436 feet tall (excluding its long aerial!). The university high-rise from 1972, designed by Herrmann Henselmann, is now an office block with a restaurant.

83

As legend will have us believe, Kloster Paulinzella owes its existence to a noblewoman named Pauline who survived an accident in the valley here. The monastic church, based on the one in Hirsau and one of the most beautiful Romanesque churches in Germany, was consecrated in 1124. The half-timbered building was where the monks held office.

The Schwarza near Bad Blankenburg. The river rises in the elevations of the Thuringian Forest, winding its way 53 kilometres or 33 miles along a narrow valley until it joins the Saale.

Right page:
The moated castle in Großkochberg was first mentioned in 1380. In 1733 it fell to the barons von Stein who then finished converting it into a baroque palace (work had begun three years previously). The central Hohes Haus rather dominates the three other wings. The small museum here documents the great love between Goethe and Charlotte von Stein.

Below:
Rudolstadt seen from the Heidecksburg. The history of the little town was determined first by the dynasty of Orlamünde and then Schwarzburg. Planned on the drawing board, the settlement was given market rights at the end of the 14th century.

Top right:
In 1599 the Schwarzburgs moved into the Heidecksburg. After the Renaissance edifice burned down it was rebuilt in baroque in two stages: from 1737 by Christoph Knöffel and from 1743 to 1756 by Gottfried Heinrich Krohne. The mighty palace now houses a museum. Its magnificent baroque interior is practically unique in Thuringia.

Centre right:
Schloss Heidecksburg seen from Rudolstadt. Friedrich Schiller lodged here in Volkstedt (now part of Rudolstadt) for a few months in 1788. To reach the house of his later wife in Rudolstadt he had to wade through the River Saale, during which, as he put it, he exposed himself to the "dangers of a sea voyage".

Bottom right:
Ice-cream parlour in Rudolstadt. The town on the Saale was first mentioned in 776 and granted a town charter in 1326.

Right:
The late Gothic town hall in Pößneck, its embellishment pre-emptive of the Renaissance period, dominates the market square. The fountain outside it with its distinctive watchman has only survived as a copy.

Bottom right page:
The road from Saalfeld to the ridge of the Thuringian Forest goes past fairy grottoes – or rather an open alum slate mine. The rich colouring of the dripstone cave is practically unique and well worth a visit.

Far left:
The town hall in Orlamünde. The great significance the town had in the Middle Ages was not ignored by early cartographers and subsequently Orlamünde could be found on any map. The counts of the same name were namely one of the most powerful noble dynasties in Germany.

Left:
Saalfeld, gateway to the Central Saale Valley, is known as the stone chronicle of Thuringia. Its Renaissance town hall is indeed splendid – and was the creation of an unusual character. Its builder was one Jakob Kelz who, although he could neither read nor write, became the town's mayor and a successful businessman to boot.

Right:
The late Gothic town hall in Neustadt an der Orla, with its ornate gables and marvellous two-storey oriel, was erected in two stages between 1495 and 1520.

Far right:
The Schweitzersches Haus in Neustadt an der Orla is also known as the Luther-haus as the Reformer is said to have stayed here when he was in town.

Right:
The Osterburg in Weida was once the seat of the vogts who gave an entire region – the Vogtland – their name. It's assumed that the castle, with its dominance of Gothic and Renaissance elements, was built on the foundations of an earlier Romanesque stronghold.

Right page:
Greiz, the 'pearl of the Vogtland', is the epitome of Germany's small states-manship. The dynasty of Reuß divided it up into Untergreiz and Obergreiz (Upper and Lower Greiz). It thus has a lower castle (Unteres Schloss), parts of which are now a museum.

Left page:
The town hall in Gera, a three-storey Renaissance edifice built between 1573 and 1576, was rebuilt following a fire in 1780. The stair tower is 57 metres or 187 feet high.

Far left:
This ornate bay window adorns the Stadtapotheke or city apothecary in Gera, a two-storey Renaissance building from the end of the 16th/beginning of the 17th centuries.

Left:
Window art. This supple figure seems little perturbed by the long drop beneath him.

Far left and left:
The entrance to the town hall in Gera was designed in the 1570s by Nicol Teiner from Lobeda and two other sculptors. The man in the archway could depict one of the mayors of that period. The identity of the lady on the front door is less ambiguous: it's the figure of Justice.

Page 96/97:
The orangery in Gera, a late baroque building with two wings, was built between 1729 and 1732 and in 1748/49. After having been used as a field hospital, stables and gymnasium, among other things, in 1972 it was turned into the city art gallery.

SKAT – THE BIRTH OF A NATIONAL PASSION

*W*andering into a German village pub of an evening, you may find a trio (usually) of men ensconced in a corner playing cards, a glass of wine or frothy Pilsner and maybe a schnapps chaser close to hand. Nothing unusual about that, you might think. But this isn't just any old game of cards. This is Skat, in Germany a pastime of religious importance in the broadest sense of the word. You may watch – but interrupt or even proffer advice at your peril! In days of yore this was regulated by specific rules, stating "Whosoever believes himself / to be so full of wisdom / that he will give the players advice / Or say / that one has not played correctly / He should be beaten about the mouth / [...] for he is an ass". You have been warned ...

Skat is an addictive game. And with exactly 2,753,294,408,504,640 ways of dealing out the cards, you'd need several lifetimes to fully sate your passion for it. In the face of such an incomprehensibly vast figure even the less mathematically adept among us can understand that games of Skat are often heated. One shudders to think what could happen if there were no proper rules and regulations governing the game – decreed by a German Skat court, no less, which has been based in Altenburg in Thuringia since 1927.

There is a very good reason why this particular town has such a great moral obligation to German society; it was namely here that Skat was devised around 200 years ago. Its inventors were of the highest calibre: a grammar school teacher, a medical official, a royal barrister, a town councillor and Chancellor Hans Karl Leopold von der Gabelentz. Their new game, which they entitled Erzgebirgischer Schafkopf or Erzgebirge Sheepshead, was an amalgam of various older games, including Wendish Sheepshead, German Solo (Modern Ombre), Tarot and Ombre. Through the *Osterländer Blätter* newspaper the public soon came to hear of this new distraction which was slowly becoming a national obsession.

Pretty ladies and bad boys

Two books of instruction and a general rule book were issued in the 1880s but this didn't solve the one essential problem of the game: the bidding system. Loyalties were divided as to whether one should play using Altenburg suits or Leipzig numbers. Differences were quickly settled as to whether to play with the French or German deck of cards, yet it took decades for a decision to be reached on a generally accepted form of bidding. In 1909, at the 10th Congress of the German Skat Federation in Leipzig, the gentlemen on the committee and the members of the society were at loggerheads. The former wanted suits, the latter numbers. The decision as to who would win the Skat battle was curiously influenced by another mass conflict: the First World War. Skat was played in the trenches where numerical bidding was preferred. A uniform system was, however, only agreed upon in 1927. Leipzig and its numbers won – but Altenburg was comforted in its defeat by the fact that it became the headquarters of the German Skat Federation.

The first championships were played in the 1930s. After the Second World War and the division of Germany into East and West, Bielefeld became the seat of the federation in the Western Sector. Only when the Berlin Wall came down were the Skat-playing fraternities of East and West reunited. At the 100th anniversary of the federation in 1999 in Altenburg the Deutscher Skatverband had over 37,000 members. In 1955 the first women's club was founded (Null Bremen) but it wasn't until 2009 that the ladies were given their own national Skat league and were finally able to compete on equal terms with the men.

You can learn about this and much more at the Skat museum in Schloss Altenburg where even those who don't consider Skat to be a vital element of their lives will find something to amuse and interest them. For example, just who has managed to make it onto a playing card: the crowned and uncrowned heads of the world, to be held in your hand; rich and powerful rulers alongside pretty ladies of various repute. And their servants, the jacks or knaves, who are usually the bad boys and the losers but who in this game can easily and very quickly tip the balance in someone else's favour ...

Left:
Pack of Saxon cards by the Bechstein brothers, Altenburg, 1935. The game of Skat originated in Altenburg in 1813 when cards like these were used.

Above:
View of the theatre in Altenburg, built in 1869/70. Incidentally, on the occasion of the XI Skat Congress in 1927 a play by local writer Otto Pech (alias Pix) was premiered with the simple yet appropriate title of "Skat".

Top right:
As you can see from these pictures, (nearly) everything in Altenburg revolves around the card game of Skat which originated here.

Centre right:
On the Skat fountain erected in Altenburg in 1903 four jacks are seen battling for supremacy.

Right:
A modern pack of cards with the French suits familiar to most English-speaking players. Where the French deck uses spades, clubs, hearts and diamonds, German playing cards have suits of hearts, bells, leaves and acorns.

99

Page 100/101:
Bird's-eye view of the market place in Altenburg which was laid out during the reign of Barbarossa around what was then a new town.

Right page:
View of the parish church dedicated to St Bartholomew in Altenburg. The aisled late Gothic hall church with its rib vault was built in the late 15th century. The mighty west tower was added in 1660–1669.

Right:
The neo-Gothic Brüderkirche in Altenburg is founded on a Franciscan monastic church from the 13th century that was torn down in 1901.

Right:
The town hall in Altenburg was erected from plans by Nikolaus Gromann between 1562 and 1564. Caspar Böschel from Chemnitz oversaw its construction. The sculptures are thought to be the work of Hermann Werner from Gotha.

Far right:
Pohlhof, the last manor house in Altenburg to have survived, was where on June 11, 1779 statesman, astronomer and arts patron Bernhard August von Lindenau first saw the light of day. His art collection formed the basis of the museum named after him.

The subject of much song and poetry – the Thuringian Forest

Winter on the Rennsteig. There are several ridges of this name in Germany. The one in Thuringia, which runs up from the valley of the Saale at Blankenstein and bends down towards the Werra at Hörschel, is not only by far the longest but also the one most shrouded in history and legend.

I love to walk along the Rennsteig through the land ..." is the roughly translated opening line of a *Heimatlied* or homeland ditty written by Karl Müller and Herbert Roth about sixty years ago which has since transcended the boundaries of Thuringia and become something of a national hit. There may be many Rennsteig Ridges but the one running along the top of the Thuringian Forest is the longest and also the one most shrouded in history and legend. The subject of much song and poetry, it has been a natural border right up to the present day. It first separated Frankish and Thuringian tribes, then the territories of various rulers whose coats of arms still pepper the wayside today. Its last divisional role was as a no-man's-land on the Saale and Werra rivers, cutting off one part of Germany from the other. Only when the two Germanys reunited was the full length of it again accessible to the general public.

The people of the Thüringer Wald, to give it its German name, have always been considered rather idiosyncratic. They think with their hearts and are full of exuberance. They tend to overexert themselves but are also straight, direct and often quite stubborn. And heated. The surroundings that form them have merely served to strengthen their individuality. Although remote villages cut off from civilisation are now a thing of the past, nearly every valley has its own dialect. The influence of Franconia can be felt south of the Rennsteig, with more Saxon creeping into vowels and consonants further north. The Thuringian Forest is not only a watershed when it comes to rainfall and the climate but also with regard to temperament. Compared to the 982 metres (3,222 feet) of the Großer Beerberg, Thuringia's highest peak, the Großer Hörselberg is a dwarf. And like the dwarf it's the stuff legend is made of. Most of the stories centre on the beautiful and seductive Venus who is said to have enticed many a mortal soul to the mountain and subsequently been their undoing ...

104

Left page:
The town hall in Arnstadt, a three-storey Renaissance building with two adjoining wings, was built at the end of the 16th century by Christoph Junghans who based his design on Dutch models.

Left:
The Liebfrauenkirche in Arnstadt from the 13th and 14th centuries is a synthesis of late Romanesque and early Gothic. The belfry was built like a late Romanesque crossing tower.

Far left:
View of the wonderful portal of the late 16th-century brewery Zum Palmbaum on the market place in Arnstadt, now a music school.

Left:
All that's left of Schloss Neideck in Arnstadt, erected in the second half of the 16th century, are the remains of the east wing and the stone tower with its baroque helm roof.

Right and right page:
The Bachkirche in Arnstadt was once called St Boniface. This was destroyed in the great fire of 1581 and not rebuilt as the Neue Kirche or new church until 1676. When Johann Sebastian Bach came to the town in 1703, he was just 18. After a brief interlude on the violin and viola in Weimar he again took up the position he loved most: seated at the organ. According to the certificate of appointment issued by Count Schwarzburg's consistory, he not only had to "suitably torment" the recently built organ in the Neue Kirche, now the Bach Church, but also had to cultivate a certain "fear of God, sobriety and acceptance".

Left page:

The mountain railway in Oberweißbach, part funicular railway, part normal-gauge electric railway, has joined Obstfelderschmiede in the Schwarza Valley with the summit station of Cursdorf since 1922.

Winter scene near Oberweißbach, the birthplace of Friedrich Fröbel (1782–1852), a pupil of Pestalozzi who founded the first kindergarten in 1840.

The grey, slate-clad houses in Lauscha creep up the slope of the narrow valley. The cradle of the glass Christmas bauble and other decorations now has a population of 3,700.

THE ORIGINS OF THE CHRISTMAS BAUBLE

Towards the end of the 16th century Christoph Müller from Bohemia and Hans Greiner from Swabia set up a glassworks in the valley of the Lauscha. In time both production and the number of families here grew to such an extent that double-barrelled surnames had to be introduced to distinguish between the many Müllers and Greiners. The forefathers of Greiner-Pol, for example, were employed at a Polish glassworks (the "Pol" standing for "Polish"), with Greiner-Schwed descended from glassworkers in Sweden; the Greiner-Bär family goes back to one Heinrich Robert who was said to have the strength of a bear (German "Bär" = English "bear"). The ancestor of Müller-Schmoß, on the other hand, had a speech defect, saying "schwos" instead of "wos" ("what") – which was duly passed down the family as "Schmoß".

The people of Lauscha are very sociable, musical and very much bound to tradition. The tiny square squashed in between the houses is not called the market place (which it actually is) but Hüttenplatz or glassworks square, which it was up until 1905 when the original glassworks had to make way for the increasing amount of traffic. The glass tubes that were made on the street provided the basic ingredients for the Christmas baubles which only started to become popular towards the end of the 19th century. Prior to their advent the trees that had gradually crept into local homes at Christmas time were decorated with fruit, sweets and brightly coloured paper.

The magic of Christmas

As the people of Lauscha had by then learnt to replicate more or less everything in the real world in glass, making tree decorations seemed a logical embellishment of their prowess. Workshops began producing in abundance, with items including houses, Father Christmases, snowmen, trumpets and trombones, birds and butterflies, fruit and nuts, icicles and pine cones, bells, balls and much more.

The tiny workshops were serviced by the entire family. Father blew into the long tubes over the flame at his glassblowing table and formed the delicate ornaments. Mother and the children dyed and painted the results. The goods were then placed on a bed of nails to dry where it was warmest, namely on special shelves rigged up to the ceiling. The rooms grew lower, the amount of gas, gold, silver and other dye solvents present in the atmosphere more dangerous. It's thus hardly surprising that glassblowers died young. The Lauscha region was one of the poorest in Germany and was for a long time an extremely deprived area. This era has thankfully passed and is almost forgotten. As are the old techniques. Many have been replaced by machines, heralding the end of the small family business.

But it's coming back. You can again watch glassblowers at work here, breathing life into any number of traditionally manufactured Christmas tree baubles. This is impressive to watch – yet the nostalgic element only truly reveals itself

Left:
The shop at the glassworks in Lauscha has several different departments; visitors are literally spoilt for choice!

Above:
Glassmaking is not just hard work; it also demands a great amount of artistic skill.

to those who appreciate how these people once lived. Life was also hard for the animals – such as the birds caught with bait and birdlime and kept in tiny, cramped cages so that their owners could have singing 'competitions' with them. The museum above Hüttenplatz eloquently documents the history of glassblowing. One rather idiosyncratic item on display is Johann Georg Greiner's glass mouth organ which he played in church every Good Friday.

If you can, you should try and visit Lauscha in the winter, when the countryside is covered in snow. This is when the magic of Christmas and of this glittering glass world really comes alive …

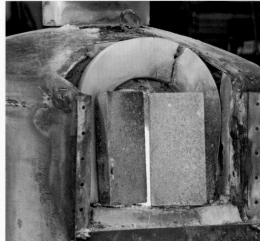

Photos, right:
At the glassworks in Lauscha tubes and rods for the glassblowers and other glass-processing trades have been made traditionally since 1853 – that is, by hand.

113

Page 114/115:
Cross-country skiers on the ridge of the Thuringian Forst near Masserberg. Well-prepared ski runs with varying degrees of difficulty can be found everywhere here.

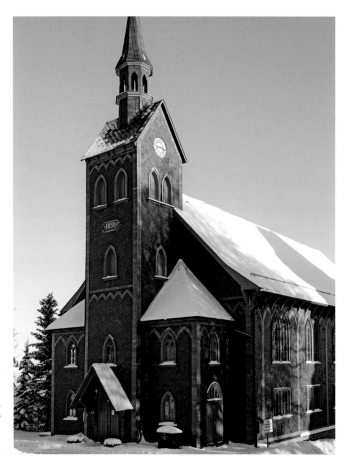

Right:
The church in the little town of Neuhaus am Rennweg, 830 metres (2,720 feet) above sea level, was consecrated in 1892 and is one of the largest wooden churches in Thuringia.

Far right:
When Masserberg's first church from 1758 was destroyed by fire, the present mountain-top place of worship was erected. This was around 120 years ago.

Right:
People have forgotten just how old the Rennsteig is – and what it was originally for. It was allegedly a trade route, yet a cart laden with goods could never have negotiated its steepest and narrowest sections. It's more probable that it was an ancient track used by messengers.

Right page:
Thanks to its curative climate Masserberg, 780 metres (2,560 feet) up on the ridge of the Thuringian Forest, has been a spa since 1999. It's also the perfect place from which to embark on hikes and cross-country skiing trips, as the Rennsteig runs right past the village.

Below:
The Rennsteig is about
170 kilometres or 105 miles
long. If you wish to cover it
all on foot or on skis, you'll
need to do so over several
days.

Top right:
As you can see, the
Schneekopf or snow summit
lives up to its name, at
978 metres (3,209 feet)
the second-highest moun-
tain in Thuringia. A new
viewing tower permits you
to view the countryside
from 1,000 metres
(3,280 feet) up.

Centre right:
Panorama Hotel in Ober-
hof. Thuringia's winter
sports resort is famous
throughout the world as

the host of many world
and European champion-
ships and various Nordic
and bob world cup events.

Bottom right:
Waiting in the wings.
The Plaue-Themar line
which runs over the top of
the Thuringian Forest is
only operated on special
train days.

Top left page:
In 1274 the Hennebergs chose the Bertholdsburg in Schleusingen as their new place of residence. The vast complex with its attractive late Renaissance façade took on its present form in the mid 16th century.

Bottom left page and photos, left:
The Henneberg museum of Kloster Veßra. The impressive Romanesque ruins in Veßra were once a monastery run by Premonstratensian canons. In 1981 the complex became an open-air museum, slowly filling with historic houses, farms and community buildings with wonderful half-timbering and painstakingly reconstructed interiors documenting how previous generations lived and worked.

Page 122/123:
The fountain on the market square in Meiningen refers to a legend, in which Emperor Heinrich II, during his stay in the town in 1003, is said to have initiated the building of the town church.

The town church dedicated to Our Blessed Lady, rebuilt in neo-Gothic between 1884 and 1889 but leaving the original Romanesque north tower and Gothic choir, dominates the old part of Meiningen.

Right page:
The neoclassical main building of the theatre in Meiningen was built in 1908/09. In the last quarter of the 19th century a theatrical group made Meiningen famous throughout Europe. The comedians from the provinces first hit Berlin on May 1, 1874 and from there went on to conquer the cities of the European continent, their performances totalling a staggering 2,592.

Schloss Elisabethenburg in Meiningen dates back to a moated castle erected by the prince-bishops of Würzburg. The former seat of the duchy of Saxe-Meiningen, founded in 1680, now accommodates Meiningen's museums, including the Max Reger archives, a café, a restaurant and the marriage suite of the local registry office.

GEORG II
DEM VOLKE
ZUR FREUDE UND ERHEBUNG

OPEN AIR

KAMMERSPIELE

SCHLOSS

ST. KIRCHE

THEATERZELT

VOLKSHAUS

SPIELRÄU 2010 - 2011

KAMMERSPIEL-PREMIEREN

PINOCCHIO
WEIHNACHTEN IM ZEL
NEUJAHRSKONZERT

CABARET

The Stadtkirche of St Georg in Schmalkalden was built between 1437 and 1509. The late Gothic church with its two steeples contains some incredible works of art, among them a Crucifixion scene from the 15th century and a carved altar and Man of Sorrows from the early 16th.

Right and right page: There are many half-timbered houses in the historic centre of Schmalkalden, one prettier than the other, some based on Hessian models and others on Franconian traditions. Schmalkalden was first governed by the Henneberg dynasty and the landgraves of Hesse. In 1583, however, it fell in its entirety to Hesse and was thus at first excluded from the federal state of Thuringia on its founding in 1920.

The Wilhelmsburg in Schmalkalden, built and named by Landgrave Wilhelm IV of Hesse, was erected in the Renaissance style between 1585 and 1589. Court sculptor Wilhelm Vernukken was partly responsible for the interior. Here, the banqueting hall.

Right page:
View through the gate of the Wilhelmsburg of the rooftops of Old Schmalkalden, with St Georg its prominent feature. In 1537 Martin Luther preached to the League of Schmalkalden in the town's late Gothic church.

128

The palace and park of Altenstein. The castle was first mentioned in 1150. Of its owners the von Hund faction has proved the most legendary; it was namely Burkhard Hund II who together with Hans von Berlepsch 'arrested' Luther, outlawed at the Imperial Diet of Worms on May 4, 1521, and took him safely to Wartburg Castle. Altenstein has been refurbished several times and was destroyed by fire in 1982. Its reconstruction should be finished by 2015.

If you want to see the most famous historical buildings in Thuringia, you don't necessarily have to travel the entire state. An alternative would be to visit the mini-a-thür park in Ruhla where models built on a scale of 1:25 depict the region's top edifices. Here, Creuzburg Castle (top) and the salt-works in Bad Salzungen (bottom).

Above:
The saltworks in Bad Salzungen, shown here in their proper size. The two elongated thorn houses are joined by a half-timbered construction in the Henneberg-Franconian style. The spa complex also has a pump room and a bandstand.

Right:
Burgsee in Bad Salzungen. Frankenstein Castle that gave the lake its name ("Burg" = castle) has almost completely disappeared. The folly of the same name, which also has a viewing tower, is from 1890.

Above:
The old border dividing the two Germanys near Geisa, the westernmost town in the former Eastern Block, is still clearly visible.

Photos, left:
The mine in Merkers, once the largest manufacturer of salt and potassium in the world, is now open to the public. The tour only takes in part of the vast underground network of pits and tunnels (totalling 4,600 kilometres or 2,860 miles!) but shows visitors a wonderful cave of crystals, the biggest and deepest concert hall in the world and the various machines and tools once used by miners.

INDEX

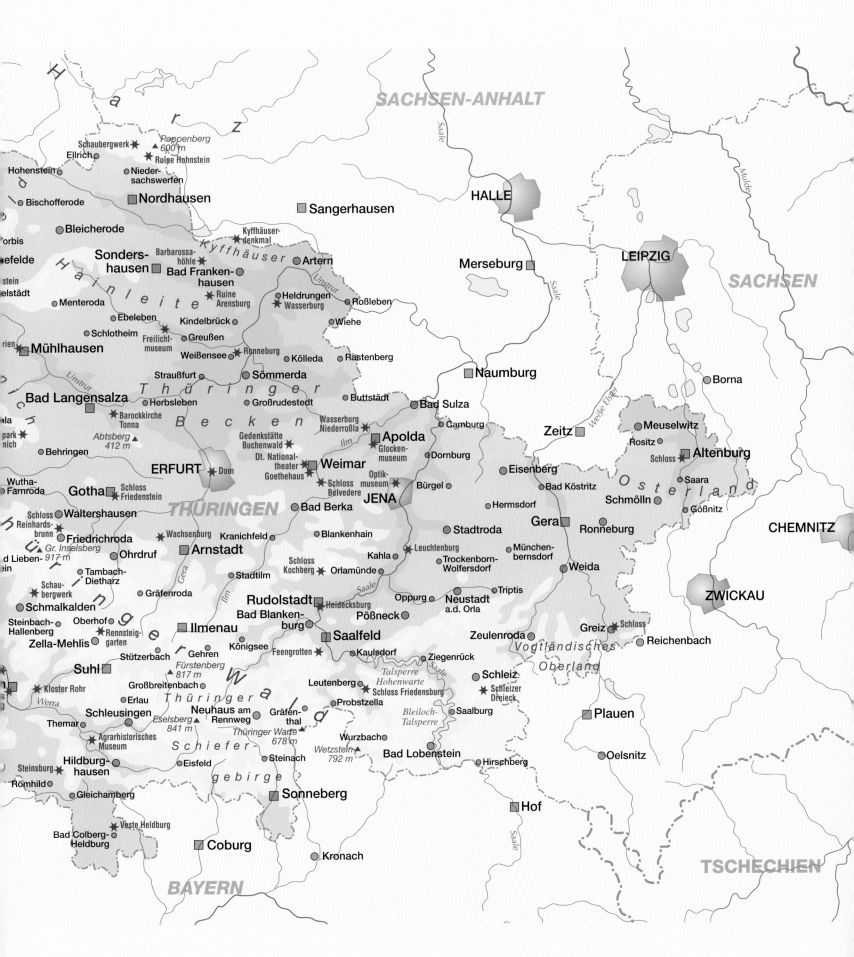

SACHSEN-ANHALT

HALLE

LEIPZIG

SACHSEN

Schaubergwerk ★
Poppenberg
▲ 600 m
Ellrich
Ruine Hohnstein ★
Hohenstein ●
Nieder- ●
sachswerfen
Saale
Bischofferode ●
■ Nordhausen
Sangerhausen ■

Bleicherode ●
Kyffhäuser-
denkmal ★
Merseburg ■
'orbis ●
Barbarossa- ★
höhle
Kyffhäuser
Artern ★
Sonders- ●
hausen
Bad Franken- ●
hausen
Unstrut
Naumburg ■
Borna ●

Menteroda ●
Ruine ★
Arensburg
Heldrungen ★
Wasserburg
Roßleben ●
Ebeleben ●
Schlotheim ●
Freilicht- ★
museum
Kindelbrück ●
Wiehe ●
Meuselwitz ●
Mühlhausen ■
Weißensee ●
Ronneburg ★
Kölleda ●
Rastenberg ●
Zeitz ■
Rositz ●
Straußfurt ●
Sömmerda ★
Bad Sulza ●
Schloss ★ Altenburg
Thüringer
Herbsleben ●
Buttstädt ●
Camburg ●
Saara ●
Bad Langensalza ■
Großrudestedt ●
Wasserburg
Niederroßla ●
Dornburg ●
Schmölln ●
Barockkirche ★
Tonna
Becken
Ilm
Apolda ●
Eisenberg ●
Gößnitz ●
Abtsberg ▲
412 m
Gedenkstätte ★
Buchenwald
Glocken- ★
museum
Bad Köstritz ●
Osterland
Behringen ●
Dt. National- ★
theater
Weimar ●
Dornburg ●
ERFURT ●
Dom ★
Goethehaus
Optik- ★
museum
Bürgel ●
Hermsdorf ●
CHEMNITZ
Gotha ●
Schloss ★
Friedenstein
Schloss ★
Belvedere
JENA ●
Gera ■
Ronneburg ●
Waltershausen ●
Bad Berka ●
Schloss ★
Reinhards-
brunn
Wachsenburg ★
Kranichfeld ●
Stadtroda ●
Weida ●
Friedrichroda ●
Blankenhain ●
München- ●
bernsdorf
Gr. Inselsberg ▲
917 m
Ohrdruf ●
Arnstadt ■
Kahla ●
Leuchtenburg ★
Trockenborn- ●
Wolfersdorf
ZWICKAU
Tambach- ●
Dietharz
Stadtilm ●
Schloss ★
Kochberg
Orlamünde ●
Triptis ●
Gera
Schau- ★
bergwerk
Gräfenroda ●
Saale
Oppurg ●
Neustadt ●
a.d. Orla
Greiz ●
Schloss ★
Reichenbach ●
Schmalkalden ●
Rudolstadt ●
Heidecksburg ★
Steinbach- ●
Hallenberg
Oberhof ●
Bad Blanken- ●
burg
Pößneck ●
Zeulenroda ●
Vogtländisches
Oberland
Zella-Mehlis ●
Rennsteig- ★
garten
Ilmenau ■
Saalfeld ■
Gehren ●
Königsee ●
Feengrotten ★
Kaulsdorf ●
Ziegenrück ●
Schleiz ●
Suhl ■
Stützerbach ●
Fürstenberg ▲
817 m
Leutenberg ●
Talsperre
Hohenwarte
Schleizer ★
Dreieck
Plauen ■
Kloster Rohr ★
Großbreitenbach ●
Schloss Friedensburg ★
Werra
Erlau ●
Thüringer Wald
Probstzella ●
Saalburg ●
Schleusingen ●
Neuhaus am ●
Rennweg
Gräfen- ●
thal
Bleiloch-
Talsperre
Oelsnitz ●
Themar ●
Eselsberg ▲
841 m
Thüringer Warte
678 m
Wurzbach ●
Agrarhistorisches ★
Museum
Wetzstein ▲
792 m
Bad Lobenstein ●
Hirschberg ●
Hildburg- ●
hausen
Eisfeld ●
Steinach ●
Steinsburg ●
Schiefer-
Römhild ●
gebirge
Gleichamberg ●
Sonneberg ●
Hof ■

Veste Heldburg ★
Bad Colberg- ●
Heldburg
Coburg ■
Kronach ●

BAYERN

TSCHECHIEN

THÜRINGEN

135

The Zeuß family out for a Sunday walk in Leimbach, a little village of 1,800 not far from Bad Salzungen.

Journey through Thuringia

Design
www.hoyerdesign.de

Map
Fischer Kartografie, Aichach

Translation
Ruth Chitty, Stromberg. www.rapid-com.de

All rights reserved
Printed in Germany
Repro by: Artilitho snc, Lavis-Trento, Italy
www.artilitho.com
Printed/Bound by Offizin Andersen Nexö, Leipzig
© 2nd edition 2015 Verlagshaus Würzburg GmbH & Co. KG
© Photos: Tina and Horst Herzig
© Text: Ernst-Otto Luthardt

ISBN 978-3-8003-4115-3

Photo credits
All photos by Tina and Horst Herzig with the exception
of the following:
page 52 (small photo), 119 (top), 131 (2 ill.), 132 (bottom),
133 (bottom, 4 ill.), 136: © Melanie Zeuß;
page 91 (top left): © Michael Sander, Wikimedia Commons
page 98 (bottom): © Gerd Matthes, www.spielkarten24.de

Details of our programme can be found at
www.verlagshaus.com